Tin

The Diary of
Earl Washington Foxwell, Jr.'s
tour of duty on the Navy Destroyer
USS Edwards DD-619
during World War II in the Pacific
September 1942 – August 1945
by **Harry J. Foxwell**

The best you can do for those who have died is to remember them.

Table of Contents

Preface	**1**
Sources and Acknowledgments	6
Other Books of Interest	11
Earl W. Foxwell, Jr.	12
About the USS Edwards, DD-619	15
Chapter 1: 1942	**19**
Timeline	20
Diary Entries and Ship Actions	23
The Ancient Order of the Deep	26
Notes and References	28
Chapter 2: 1943	**29**
Timeline	30
Diary Entries and Ship Actions	31
Notes and References	47
Chapter 3: 1944	**49**
Timeline	50
Diary Entries and Ship Actions	51
Legion of Merit Award	52
The Kamikazes	65
Notes and References	77
Chapter 4: 1945	**79**
Timeline	80
Diary Entries and Ship Actions	81
Notes and References	92
Epilog	**93**
Appendix	**94**
About the Author	**99**

Preface

As the Empire of Japan grew in strength and ambition under Emperor Showa (Hirohito) in the early part of the 20th Century, it coveted access to the raw materials needed for industrial and economic growth – oil, rubber, and iron – which were scarce on the Japanese Islands but plentiful in China, Korea, and other parts of Asia. Japan had already occupied Manchuria and other parts of Northern China, which severely strained relations between the two Asian nations. Using a minor conflict in July 1937 between their armies at the Marco Polo Bridge near Beijing as an excuse for all out war, Japan escalated the fighting into a full-scale invasion of China.

In reaction to Japan's aggressiveness, the US and its allies responded by freezing Japanese assets and halting oil shipments in an attempt to convince Japan to end its invasion of China; at the time the US supplied nearly 80% of Japan's oil needs. Japan, already allied with Germany, refused to exit China and concluded it would need to go to war with the US, whom they saw as an impediment to their plans to conquer more of Asia.

In one of the most successful surprise attacks in military history, Japanese aircraft attacked the US Navy fleet at Pearl Harbor, Hawaii on Sunday, December 7, 1941. President Franklin D. Roosevelt's announcement of the attack set the stage for the nearly four-year long naval and land conflict with Japan in the Pacific Ocean:

1

"Yesterday, December seventh, 1941, a date which will live in infamy, the United States of America was suddenly and deliberately attacked by naval and air forces of the Empire of Japan. We will gain the inevitable triumph, so help us God."

In spite of the apparent success of that attack, Japan had serious misgivings about the events they had set into motion. Admiral Isoroku Yamamoto, chief architect of the attack on Pearl Harbor, reportedly admitted "I fear all we have done is to awaken a sleeping giant and fill him with a terrible resolve." And he further commented on the future of the path he had chosen: "I can run wild for six months...after that I have no expectation of success". The Imperial Japanese Army and Navy did indeed "run wild" for a time, invading and capturing the Philippine Islands, Malaya, Singapore, Hong Kong, the Dutch East Indies, and numerous other Pacific Islands.

The US military's goal in response to Japan's aggression was the complete destruction of the Imperial Japanese Navy and Army, and Japan's unconditional surrender. To accomplish this goal, General Douglas MacArthur and Admiral Chester Nimitz devised the plan known as "island hopping" – capturing islands ever closer to Japan and using them as air and land bases for further advancement. This strategy involved naval bombardment of Japanese-held islands by offshore ships and fighter-bombers, as well as full-scale beach landings and invasions by thousands of Army and Marine troops. Among the first such islands was Tarawa in November 1943 using the 2nd Marine Division supported by bombardment from Navy ships including the **USS Edwards**. That engagement succeeded in three days although more than 1000 Marines were killed and more than 2000 wounded. But later island battles would prove far more difficult. Continuing into 1944, combined Marine and Navy attacks hit the heavily fortified islands of Kwajalein and Eniwetok, Truk, Saipan, Guam, and Tinian, and ultimately the Philippines, Iwo Jima, and Okinawa where more than 14,000 US soldiers and 77,000 Japanese soldiers died.

The Battle of Okinawa was one of the largest amphibious assaults of the Pacific war, and lasted nearly 3 months, supported by continuous fire support from US Navy gunships, again including the **USS Edwards**. Its capture provided key military bases for the final planned assault on Japan itself, only a few hundred miles away. The fall of Okinawa, along with the near total destruction of the Imperial Navy and the atomic bombings of Hiroshima and Nagasaki, led Japan to unconditionally surrender on September 2, 1945, a date now known as "VJ Day" (Victory over Japan Day).

In the later part of the Pacific naval war against Japan, US Navy destroyers and destroyer escorts were often deployed on anti-Kamikaze "picket duty" along with constant carrier-based air patrols – early warning visual and radar detection of incoming attacking aircraft in order to protect the larger ships. These destroyers were usually the first ships to be attacked by the suicide pilots; picket duty during the Okinawa campaign in 1945 for example was among the most dangerous of destroyer missions.

This book tells of one such destroyer, the **USS Edwards**, and one young sailor, **Earl W. Foxwell, Jr.**, through the words of his war diary.

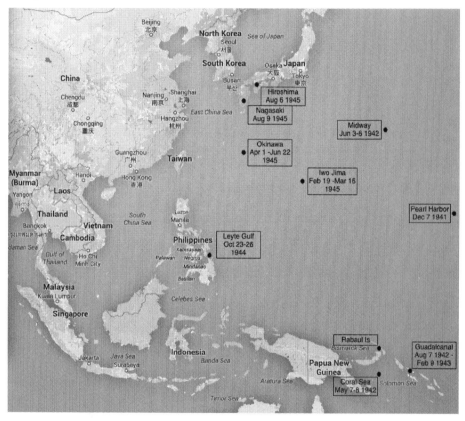

Map of the Western Pacific Ocean conflict area
during World War II, 1941-1945
Google Map annotation by the author.

The *Enola Gay* B-29 that dropped the atomic bomb on Hiroshima. Photo by the author of this historic aircraft on display at the Smithsonian's *Udvar-Hazy National Air and Space Museum* in Chantilly, Virginia.

Sources and Acknowledgements

In February 2013, as the result of a few odd coincidences and some random Web browsing, I discovered online information about the US Navy destroyer *USS Edwards DD-619*. My father, *Earl Washington Foxwell, Jr.*, served on that ship in the Pacific during World War II from September 1942 through October 1945. Additionally, a "family heirloom" -- my father's war diary – was kept partially preserved and was now in my possession, albeit written in very hard to read and fading pencil script [1].

David Collins of San Francisco, whose father also served on the Edwards, was kind enough to send me additional information about that ship, including an abbreviated, informal copy of its war record from 18 September 1942 through 15 August 1945. That document appears to be derived from the ship's Action Reports, Deck Logs, and personal accounts.

First page of Earl's war diary

The *Nimitz Library* at the US Naval Academy in Annapolis, Maryland archives Action Reports for many of the ships that fought in World War II, including those for the **USS Edwards**; I have obtained and included herein material from these archives.

The National Archives and Records Administration in College Park, Maryland houses additional material related to US Navy operations during World War II, including photographs and Deck Logs for the participating ships. I have included some material from these records, although such logs contain primarily administrative and navigation details while the separate Action Reports are more informative.

As a result of this fortunate coming together of historical sources, I have merged the diary entries, where possible, with the ship's log, Action Reports, and with other resources and commentary, to produce this chronicle of the **USS Edwards'** and Earl's wartime experiences. It is not meant to be a complete history of the US Navy's and **USS Edwards'** campaigns in the Pacific, nor is it a full biography. Rather, it is a mere glimpse of that part of the war through one very young sailor's perspective.

Entries in **bold font** marked "**EWF: mm/dd/yr**" are direct transcriptions from Earl's diary, and generally attempt to preserve his spelling and grammar, although I have corrected when possible his spellings of place names and US Navy warships. I have included all of his entries to provide a complete sense of a sailor's view of the war action and daily activities especially when he did not grasp the full context of the ship's orders. Selected entries labeled "NDWD: mm/dd/yr" are from the *Navy Day October 27, 1945 War Diary of the USS Edwards* [2]. Selected entries labeled "AR:mm/dd/yr" are from the declassified *US Navy Action Reports of the USS Edwards (DD-619)* now archived in the *Nimitz Library*. Special thanks to Dr. Jennifer Bryan, Head of Special Collections, for providing access to these documents.

Included among the chapter Notes and References are items identified as "family lore". These notes are from the author's recollection of post-war comments and discussions by Earl and other family members.

Much of this material involved transcribing entries from the diary and other printed documents. I have almost certainly made errors in the transcriptions, and, having been an Army Infantry "grunt" unfamiliar with naval terminology, I have probably failed to use proper US Navy terms in some of the descriptions. My apologies to the US Navy!

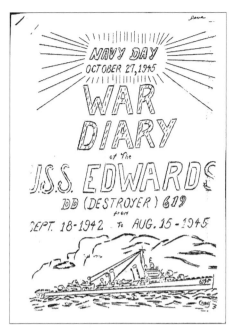

Cover pages of the Edwards' Navy Day War Diary, from Oct 27, 1945

Other Books of Interest

While writing and researching for this book, I discovered numerous others of greater length and content that describe the battles in the Pacific and the Kamikaze attacks. Several of these include personal experience details based on interviews with surviving sailors. I highly recommend these to readers interested in a more comprehensive coverage of that period:

- *At War with the Wind,* David Sears, 2008: http://www.amazon.com/At-War-Wind-David-Sears-ebook/dp/B0073GUVTO/
- *Neptune's Inferno: The U.S. Navy at Guadalcanal,* James D. Hornfischer, 2011: http://www.amazon.com/Neptunes-Inferno-U-S-Navy-Guadalcanal/dp/0553385127
- *The Last Stand of the Tin Can Sailors,* James D. Hornfischer, 2004: http://www.amazon.com/The-Last-Stand-Sailors-Extraordinary/dp/0553381482/
- *The Battle of Leyte Gulf: 23-26 October 1944,* Thomas J. Cutler, 2014: http://www.amazon.com/The-Battle-Leyte-Gulf-Bluejacket/dp/1557502439/
- *Kamikaze Attacks of World War II,* Robin L. Rielly, 2010 : http://www.amazon.com/Kamikaze-Attacks-World-War-II/dp/0786473037

Earl W. Foxwell, Jr.

Pencil/charcoal sketch of Earl by artist Jack Logan, circa 1945 [3]

Uniform patch for Earl's rating, Fire Controlman 3rd Class.

DOB: 7/20/26, Cape Charles, VA [4], Died: 12/31/71

USN: #6587989, July '42 - Oct '45
      Fire Controlman, 3c [5] [6]

Enlisted: 7/29/42, Discharged: 12/6/45

Earl enlisted in the US Navy on July 29, 1942; he boarded the destroyer **USS Edwards** on September 19, 1942, a mere seven weeks later, supposedly trained for life at sea and naval combat aboard a small, vulnerable warship. He was sixteen years old.

[1] Author's Note: I photographed the diary entries and examined the images using my computer (Apple & iPhoto) in order to read the faded pencil script. This allowed for enlarging the text and adjusting the contrast to enhance readability. In some cases, the diary pages had to be viewed under ultraviolet light to reveal the text. Where some words were illegible, I have made reasonable guesses based on the other references.

[2] After the official end of the war, there were several "Navy Day" celebrations around the US held on October 27, 1945. These events included the return of ships to their home or namesake ports, and included a special address in New York City by then President Harry S. Truman. The **USS Edwards** took part in one of these events and a "War Diary" of the ship was prepared and distributed. There is no author indicated on this document.

Navy Day Address (October 27, 1945), Harry S. Truman,
http://millercenter.org/president/speeches/detail/3342

[3] Family lore suggests Logan was one of Earl's crewmates.
(perhaps
http://www.haysmemorial.com/obits/obituary.php?id=337175 ?)

[4] Family lore relates that Earl's mother, nee Artie L. Firesheets,
certified to the local recruiting office that Earl was old enough (17)
to enlist in 1942. His Navy Notice of Separation lists his birth date
as 20 July 1925. In a later document – an application for
employment at a DoD contractor in his own handwriting – he lists
his birth date as 20 July 1926.

[5] U.S. Navy World War II Enlisted Rates:
http://uniform-
reference.net/insignia/usn/usn_ww2_enl_seaman.html

[6] Bud Kahlenbeck, who also served on the Edwards, relates that
Earl served in the CIC (Combat Information Center);
see http://www.destroyers.org/inside-story/is-cic1.htm

About the USS Edwards, DD-619

The *USS Edwards* was a Destroyer class warship of the United States Navy during World War II. Destroyers were originally designed to counter attacks by the small, fast, enemy torpedo patrol boats that preyed on the larger "capital ships" – battleships and aircraft carriers. Destroyer crewmen typically called their ships "cans" (short for "tin cans"), supposedly because of their thin armor, although that did make the ships light and fast.

The *USS Edwards* was named for Lieutenant Commander Walter A. Edwards (1886–1926), who as commander of the *USS Bainbridge* in 1922 rescued nearly five hundred people from the burning French transport *Vinh-Long*. For his heroism Edwards was awarded the U.S. Medal of Honor, the French Légion d'honneur, and the British Distinguished Service Order.

The Edwards, a *Gleaves Class* destroyer, was launched on 19 July 1942 by Federal Shipbuilding and Drydock Company, Kearny, New Jersey. She was longer than a football field and carried a crew of more than 200 men. Her armament included .50-caliber machine guns, five-inch anti-aircraft cannons, 21-inch torpedoes and depth charges, and she could cruise at more than 37 knots (40 mph).

The Edwards and her crew received 14 Battle Star citations for their World War II service.

A Destroyer's *Combat Information Center* showing the ship's radar console and fire control computer.
Photo copyright Tin Can Sailors, Inc. Used with permission.

A destroyer's Combat Information Center (CIC) was a small, cramped area which housed the ship's radar displays and fire control computers. Its job was to identify and communicate potential air and sea threats, collecting and coordinating radio, visual, radar, and sonar information, and to direct the ship's large guns. The destroyer's radar provided early warning for the ship itself and, while on "picket duty", for the larger carriers and cruisers. The Edwards' Deck Logs recorded frequent problems with the radar system.

As an example of how the CIC was used, here is a sample from the log of another destroyer:

The performance of the CIC was of inestimable value in handling the ship during the engagement. All navigation of the ship was accomplished from the CIC. When the ship originally came under fire, bearings were taken on the flashes, sent to the CIC, and then from there data selected on known targets and the probable batteries taken under fire, using the gunnery officer as a spotter. For the bombardment of the shore positions CIC furnished the data and controlled the indirect fire, using the gunnery officer only for the spotter. When the air bombardment commenced and there was considerable flak from AA batteries, CIC was able to give advice as to whether flashes were from known gun locations or whether it was probable AA fire. This information was of great value in preventing the taking of needless targets under fire.

From the Log of the USS Corry, in *United States Destroyer Operations in World War II*, Theodore Roscoe, 1960, Naval Institute Press, pg 349.

U.S.S. EDWARDS (DD619)

The U.S.S. Edwards (DD619) was launched 19 July 1942 by Federal Shipbuilding and Drydock Co., Kearney, N.J. and commissioned 18 September 1942. After very active duty in the Pacific, covering almost a half million miles, was placed in the inactive fleet in Charleston S.C. 11 April 1946. While in the Pacific, the U.S.S. Edwards (DD619) had 17 confirmed downing of enemy aircraft, 6 major amphibious landings, and was credited with sinking 1 enemy submarine. The U.S.S. Edwards (DD619) was awarded 14 Battle Stars for WWII service, all without suffering any casualties to the personnel.

**THIS PLAQUE IS DEDICATED TO THE U.S.S. EDWARDS (DD619)
TO ALL WHO STOOD THE WATCHES, MANNED THE BATTLE STATIONS AND ...**

CDR. Paul G. Osler, Legion of Merit Medal   LCDR. Simon E. Ramey, Silver Star Medal

Navy & Marine Corps Medal and the Bronze Star Medal recipients:

Lt. Frank Mann, CPhM Emery Pensak, MoMM 1/C Frank A.S. Elliott,
SM2/C John J. Crane, Cox James J. Gonsalves and S1/C Richard Stanley.

PRESENTED BY THE U.S.S. EDWARDS (DD619) ASSOCIATION 25 OCTOBER 2002

Photograph: Plaque dedicated to USS Edwards,
Navy Day, 29 October 2002

See also:

Dictionary of American Naval Fighting Ships – Index,
http://www.history.navy.mil/research/histories/ship-histories/danfs.html

USS Edwards, DD-619,
http://www.history.navy.mil/research/histories/ship-histories/danfs/e/edwards-ii.html

Chapter 1: 1941-1942

Timeline

1941

December

7	Japan attacks Pearl Harbor, Wake, Guam, Midway, and other Pacific islands
8	US and Britain declare war on Japan
10	Japan attacks Luzon, Philippines
7-23	Battle of Wake Island

1942

January

2	Japan captures Manila, Philippines
7	Japan attacks Bataan
23	Japan captures Rabaul and Bougainville islands

February

1	US carriers Yorktown and Enterprise attack Gilbert and Marshall islands
22	President FDR orders General MacArthur out of Philippines
26	US carrier Langley sunk
27	Allied defeat in Battle of Java Sea

March

24	Admiral Nimitz appointed CINC of Pacific Theater

April

9	US forces on Bataan surrender to Japanese
18	Doolittle's surprise bombing raid on Tokyo

May

6	Japanese troops take Corregidor, US troops surrender
7-8	Japanese Navy defeated in Battle of Coral Sea

June

4-7	Battle of Midway, major defeat for JIN: US planes from carriers Enterprise, Hornet, and Yorktown destroy Japanese carriers, USS Yorktown carrier sunk

August

7	US Marines land on Guadalcanal
24	Japanese Navy carriers defeated at Battle of Eastern Solomons

September

15	Japanese warships sink US carrier Wasp and destroyer O'Brien

October

26	US carrier Hornet lost in Battle of Santa Cruz

November

12-14	Naval battle at Guadalcanal

Japan had awakened America from its somewhat isolationist slumber; the day after the Pearl Harbor attack, the US Congress declared war on Japan. In response to the shock of the attack, with a combination of a compulsory draft and voluntary enlistments, more than 8 million citizens joined the US Army and more than one million joined the US Navy.

The post-attack draft required every able-bodied man aged 18 to 65 to register for potential military service, although thousands of men enthusiastically volunteered. Volunteers 17 years old needed parental permission to enlist.

On December 7, 1941, **Earl Washington Foxwell, Jr**. was not yet 16 years old. But about a week after his 16th birthday he enlisted in the US Navy on July 29, 1942, apparently with the validation by his mother that he was old enough. By the time of his enlistment, the war in the Pacific was well under way; Japan's empire stretched from Manchuria through South East Asia to New Guinea and countless Pacific Islands.

The US had already attacked Tokyo with *Doolittle's Raid*, defeated the Japanese Navy at the battles of Coral Sea, Midway, and Eastern Solomons. Yet nearly three more bloody years of naval and island warfare lie ahead for Earl and the **USS Edwards**. While the ship was being built and Earl was in his basic Navy training, the Marine and Navy campaign to retake Guadalcanal Island got underway and would not end for nearly six months. The Edwards and her crew would see their first combat action in January of 1943 in support of that effort.

Diary Entries and Ship Actions

The *USS Edwards DD-619* is commissioned, and Earl's diary begins:

NDWD: 18 SEP 42

    USS Edwards commissioned at Navy Yard, NY, NY

NDWD: 18 SEP 42 – 1 OCT 42

    Post-Commissioning fitting out period at New York, NY

As Earl was preparing to board the newly commissioned destroyer that was to be his home at sea for the next three years, half a world away on the island of Guadalcanal the US Marines were fighting the Battle of Bloody Ridge, one of the fiercest ground engagements of the Pacific war and a key turning point in the campaign against Japan. In a few short months, Earl and the *USS Edwards* would be at the island supporting the final stages of the American victory over the Japanese there. His first diary entry is for September 19, 1942.

EWF: Sept 19/42

    Diary of U.S.S. Edwards...went in commission. I went aboard that day.

EWF: Oct 2/42

    Edwards starts trial runs. Rams a Limy tanker [1]. Went back in Dry Dock for repair

EWF: Oct 9/42

The Edwards goes on her trial runs to Portland Maine.

NDWD: 9 OCT 42 – 31 OCT 42

Shakedown at Casco Bay, Maine

EWF: Nov 8/42

Returned from Portland Maine to Brooklyn NY

NDWD: 8 NOV 42 – 11 DEC 42

Convoy duty east coast and Caribbean Sea.

EWF: Nov 15/42

I went to gunners school. Went home from school…Stayed overleave 2 days and missed the ship.

Earl's official Service Record shows that he was "Declared a Straggler"* and "Absent Over Leave" on 7 Nov 42, with "Intentions Unknown". His personal effects were "inventoried and placed in safe keeping" on the ship; the Navy offered a $25 reward for his return. He surrendered himself to the Navy facility in Brooklyn NY on 9 Nov 42 and was returned to Norfolk VA for "disciplinary action". He was confined to the ship for 20 days and had his $50/month pay reduced by $20/month; he did not record any of these details in his diary.

* A "straggler" is a person or ship that "becomes separated" from their unit, a typical designation for sailors who have overstayed their official leave time and fail to return to their ship on time.

EWF: Nov 11/42

    Edwards starts for Virgin Islands

EWF: Nov 28/42

    <u>Boy what a time</u>. **Edwards returns to States from Virgin Islands.**

EWF: Dec 4/42

    Little we knew how long this old can would be away from the states this time

NDWD: 11 DEC 42 – 12 DEC 42

    Transited Panama Canal to Pacific Ocean.

NDWD: 12 DEC 42 – 4 JAN 43

    Enroute Panama Canal Zone to Noumea, New Caledonia in company with Task Group consisting of cruisers, escort carriers and destroyers.

EWF: Dec 14/42

    We crossed the equator. "Did us Pollywogs catch hell!"

The first time a sailor crosses the Equator while aboard ship is a momentous event accompanied by much ceremony and a bit of hazing. This tradition dates back at least to the early 1800's and was practiced by the British Royal Navy as well as by Spanish, Portuguese, Dutch, and Italian navies and merchant ships.

Sailors who had not yet experienced their first "Line Crossing" were called "Pollywogs" and were subjected to taunts, tricks, dunking, extra work tasks, and in earlier days even beatings and near drowning. Upon completing the "ceremony", sailors were promoted to "Shellbacks", or "Sons of Neptune", and received an award or certificate. US Navy sailors during WW II received a membership card for the "Ancient Order of the Deep", signed by "His Majesty' Scribe, Davy Jones", and by "Neptunus Rex, Ruler of the Raging Main".

On 14 December 1942, Earl received his membership in the Order, and participated in the crossing ceremonies with several of his crewmates.

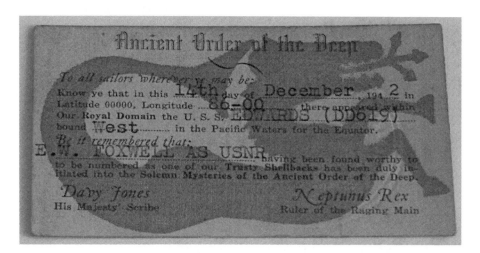

Author's photo of Earl's *Order of the Deep* membership card.

EWF: Dec 25/42

I hope I never have another Xmas day like today

[End of 1942 diary entries]

Notes and References

[1] Collision between USS Edwards (DD-619) and British Steamship *SS Empire Mouflon.* Occurred in Gravesend Bay, New York Harbor, October 2 1942.

http://research.archives.gov/description/4687009

Chapter 2: 1943

Timeline

1943

January
29   USS Chicago sunk, *USS Edwards* rescues 224 crew members

February
1   Japanese begin evacuation of Guadalcanal

April
18   Japanese Admiral Yamamoto dies in allied air attack

May
11-30 Battle of Attu

August
2   John F. Kennedy's PT-109 sunk
15   Battle of Kiska

Diary Entries and Ship Actions

EWF: Jan 1/43

　　We crossed the international date line. And we did not have a new years day.

EWF: Jan 5/43

　　Reached New Caledonia.

EWF: Jan 24/43

　　The Old Edwards had her first taste of the war. 9 Jap torpedo planes attacked us. They put 3 fish* in the Chicago.

　　* torpedoes were called "fish"

NDWD: 29 JAN 43

　　Attacked by seven (7) to nine (9) torpedo planes and bombers during night. No planes shot down, USS CHICAGO (CA-29) damaged by torpedo and taken in tow by USS LOUISVILLE (CA-28).

AR: 30 JAN 43

　　...SC radar picked up formation of unidentified aircraft bearing about 300, distant about 30 miles...at about 1925, starboard side of formation commenced firing. Went to General Quarters. Planes were very difficult to see against clouds and to the eastward except occasionally in light of A.A. tracers. One plane crossed ahead of EDWARDS rather close aboard, strafing from rear cockpit...At one time during the attack, three splashes, such as might be made by 50 or 100 pound bombs or shells, were observed about 1500 yards on the starboard beam, well clear of all ships.

...All personnel...performed their duties in a very cool and deliberate manner. This was the first time under enemy fire for all but a very few of the ship's personnel. The conduct of all subordinates was exemplary.

EWF: Jan 30/43

Again the Japs attacked us. This time they sank the Chicago. The Edwards got 5 of the planes in all.

NDWD: 30 JAN 43

At 1620 eleven (11) twin engine Japanese torpedo planes attacked crippled USS CHICAGO (CA-29), now being towed by USS NAVAHO (AT-64). USS CHICAGO (CA-29) hit again in action and abandoned and sunk. USS LAVALLETTE (DD-448) damaged and under tow. USS EDWARDS (DD-619) destroyed five (5) of the attacking planes and sustained no personnel or material damage. Picked up 224 USS CHICAGO (CA-29) survivors.

NDWD: 30 JAN 43 – 1 FEB 43

Escorted USS LAVALLETTE (DD-448) towed by USS NAVAHO (AT-64) to Luganville Bay, Espiritu Santo, New Hebrides.

EWF: Feb 12/43

Went back to the same place the Chicago was sunk. We operated 35 miles South of Guadalcanal

EWF: Mar 20/43

We left Havannah Harbor. Heading for Pearl Harbor.

EWF: Mar 27/43

We reached Pearl Harbor. Had a very nice Liberty.

EWF: Apr 15/43

We left Pearl Harbor for Adak, in the Aleutian Islands.

EWF: Apr 30/43

We arrived in Adak

EWF: May 1/43

We got underway to meet some cruisers and cans.

EWF: May 11/43

United States war ships bombarded and landed troops on Attu Island

EWF: May 12/43

The Edwards contacted a sub. At 12:35 on May 13 we had depth charged it to the surface and sunk it.

NDWD: May 12-13

While off of Attu attacked submarine which fired torpedo at USS Pennsylvania (BB-38). USS Edwards (DD-619) and USS Farragut (DD-348) conducted attacks from evening until early morning and attacks ended when submarine surfaced and was taken under fire by USS Edwards (DD-619). Submarine subsequently disappeared. Assessed class "B" kill.

For this action the Commanding Officer, Commander Paul G. OSLER, USN received the Legion of Merit medal.

EWF: May 16/43

We go into Adak harbor for more charges and ammunition

EWF: May 16/43

At 8:00 we get underway for operations between Japan and the Aleutian Chain

[No diary entries until June 25]

EWF: Jun 25/43

While the Frazier and Monaghan were patrolling 8000 yards of Kiska, each one got a sub. We relieved them in the morning of June 18. We got two air contacts but they were our planes bombing Kiska.

EWF: Jun 26/43

We are relieved from patrol and go into harbor for some well deserved rest. There seems to be a big force gathering up here. Some of the boys say there will more than likely be a big Naval battle.

EWF: Jun 27/43

We get under way for patrol around Kiska again

EWF: Jul 6/43

We are relieved from patrol around Kiska

EWF: Jul 9/43

We start out with cruisers for patrol

EWF: Jul 15/43

We are only 1400 miles from San F. I don't think we will go any closer than that though.

EWF: Jul 16/43

I was night*, we changed course from 180 to 320. Looks like were going back to Adak

* Night Watch

EWF: Jul 19/43

We refueled from a tanker. We expect to be back in Adak by 23.

EWF: Jul 22/43

We arrived in port today one day ahead of time. We refueled and took on stores. Were going out with another big force. We don't know what is up yet but we will know soon enough.

EWF: Jul 25/43

For the last few days it has been clear and sunny. The best days we have had for 3 months.

EWF: Jul 26/43

Something must be cooking up here. We saw a force of our Battle wagons while we were patrolling North West of Attu.

EWF: Jul 28/43

A fish was fired at us tonight around 2:30. And the battle ships picked up a surface contact. We went out to investigate but we picked up nothing.

EWF: Aug 2/43

We (the Edwards) along with the cruisers and battle wagons gave Kiska a heavy bombardment while B-24s dropped bombs on them.

EWF: Aug 8/43

It looks like tomorrow will be the invasion of Kiska. We have the biggest fleet up here now than we did when the war started.

EWF: Aug 9/43

I was wrong but I know it won't be long.

EWF: Aug 12/43

We (the Edwards) along with other war ships bombarded hell out of Kiska.

EWF: Aug 15/43

Today American troops landed on Kiska and met no enemy resistance during the landing

EWF: Aug 24/43

Today we left that God forsaken place in the Aleutians and headed for the States

EWF: Aug 31/43

We hit Frisco after 9 long months of war. What a time.

EWF: Sep 2/43

We start for Bremerton, Wash.

EWF: Sep 4/43

We arrived in Bremerton, Wash.

EWF: Sep 26/43

We left Bremerton and went to Seattle

EWF: Sep 28/43

We left Seattle. We don't know where we will put into port next. Boy did this crew really raise hell in Seattle.

EWF: Sep 28/43

5:30 The skipper just announced our next destination would be Pearl Harbor.

EWF: Oct 3/43

We arrived at Pearl Harbor

EWF: Oct 6/43

We went out with the Bunker Hill for practice runs

EWF: Oct 9/43

We came back into Pearl Harbor

EWF: Oct 11/43

7:45 The Captain first passed the word we were under way for Espiritu Santo. That is the place we took the survivors of the Chicago. We went out with the carrier Princeton.

EWF: Oct 12/43

We sure have been giving the Pollywogs a going over today. A couple more days and they will really get it.

EWF: Oct 15/43

I actually felt sorry for these guys today. They took more punishment than the old gang took when we crossed for the first time.

EWF: Oct 16/43

We fueled from the Princeton

EWF: Oct 20/43

We arrived in Espiritu Santo in the South West Pacific. Most all the ships in here have Jap flags on them. I'll bet we see some real action now.

EWF: Oct 22/43

We pulled out this morning with the Saratoga, Princeton, San Juan, San Diego, Buchanan, and Woodworth.

EWF: Oct 22/43

[deleted entry]

EWF: Oct 29/43

We left Espiritu Santo with 8 cans 2 cruisers 2 carriers. Something is in the wind.

EWF: Oct 30/43

At 4:05 this morning we were at G.Q.* for Drill. It came over the phones that this task force would lend air support while troops landed on Bougainville Island. We were told to expect any kind of resistance.

* G.Q. means "General Quarters". That is, "Battle Stations"; prepare for battle or imminent damage

EWF: Nov 1/43

At 5:24 this morning our planes took off to make bombing raids on the Jap held island Bougainville. We are at least 100 miles from the island. We are also in Jap controlled waters.

EWF: Nov 1/43

They just announced that the first raid was successful.
But we lost 3 planes in the attack.

EWF: Nov 1/43

Around 12:45 the planes made another attack on the
fields without loss of any planes. They killed off plenty of Japs.

EWF: Nov 2/43

We first heard that our light cruiser force beat hell out of
the Japs. They used radar control all night and this morning
they were attacked by (70) seventy torpedo bombers. The
Denver and Foot got hit but they drove off the planes.

EWF: Nov 2/43

We will fuel most all day today. Tomorrow we will make
more bombing raids on Bougainville.

EWF: Nov 3/43

We won't pull any more raids on Bougainville. We are
going to bomb Rabaul.

EWF: Nov 4/43

We are about 150 miles from Rabaul. We will pull our
attack in the morning.

EWF: Nov 5/43

We had complete air coverage today while all our carrier planes took off on the attack on Rabaul at 5:52. We have our colors at half mast in memorial for the men we lost today.

EWF: Nov 8/43

We came into port today. Admiral Halsey said we sure gave the Japs hell on Rabaul in our last attacks. He said it was the most successful action since Midway and he congratulated all hands in Task Force 38 (in which the Edwards is a part).

EWF: Nov 8/43

We pulled out this afternoon with 2 carriers and 9 cans. The names are (carriers) New Livingston(?) and Bunker Hill. (cans) Murray, Chelsea, Kidd, McKay, Edwards, and I forget the rest.

EWF: Nov 11/43

This morning we pulled the raid on Rabaul with a couple hundred planes. One of the fighters couldn't get his wheels down to land on the carrier. So he crashed his plane and we picked him up. We asked him how it was over Rabaul. I quote him "I was too busy with the zeros* to notice anything else." His name is Parker (Lieutenant Parker). He said he shot down two zeros.

* The Japanese "Zero" fighter plane

EWF: Nov 11/43

At 1:50 we went to general quarters. Because the carriers picked up a group of planes on radar about 72 miles away. At 2:15 jap planes attacked us. There were dive bombers and torpedo planes. Boy was it a fight. We got 2 planes in all. The boys expect them back tonight. But I think they have enough of our fighters for awhile. In all there were 150 some planes that attacked. The biggest attack since the battle of Santa Cruz.

NDWD: Nov 11/43

At noon about thirty (30) Vals* attacked the task group. In the ensuing action the USS Edwards (DD-619) shot down two (2) planes and assisted in the destruction of two (2) more with no material or personnel damage to herself.

* Japanese Aichi Dive Bomber

EWF: Nov 16/43

They just announced our next destination would be Pearl Harbor. We are to destroy an airfield in the Gilbert Islands so we can land troops. We have with us 2 carriers 2 cruisers 7 cans.

EWF: Nov 18/43

Our planes took off this morning at 3:00 o'clock to bomb Manus. They returned about 9:30 and reported the raid very successful. They say there are going to be 19 carriers 14 B.B. 36 c 60 DD and several hundred different airplanes in this drive. We are in Task Group 50.4.

NDWD: Nov 19/43

Night snooper shot at with no success.

EWF: Nov 22/43

We haven't met up with the other force yet. We were supposed to meet them this evening but we didn't.

EWF: Nov 23/43

We met the group of ships today at 5:45. There were 19 ships in all. There were tankers transports and (DE's)

EWF: Nov 24/43

About 7:00 o'clock 2 more cruisers and 2 more cans joined us. That makes about 30 ships all total. I think this is reinforcements for the Gilbert Islands campaign.

EWF: Nov 24/43

We separated from the rest of the ships. We're with the same group as before.

EWF: Nov 25/43

We joined up with another force today. There was the Indiana, Massachusetts, North Carolina, Enterprise, and a few other carriers and cans.

EWF: Nov 28/43

At 18:25 this evening we went to general quarters. The radar picked up some boogies (enemy planes) 27 miles out. They came in just to snoop I guess cause they went back out and lost them on radar at 19:15. I think we are now headed for Pearl Harbor.

EWF: Nov 30/43

I was wrong. We, the Gansevoort and another can left the other ships and headed for Tarawa in the Gilbert Islands. The Battle of Tarawa is the most brilliant page in Marine History.

EWF: Dec 1/43

We arrived at Tarawa at about 12:15 but we didn't go in. Boys this island sure looks like it took a beating.

EWF: Dec 1/43

We went in tonight at 18:30 to give one of the LST's 10,000 gal. of water for the troops. I got a page out of a Jap book for a souvenir.

EWF: Dec 2/43

We left Tarawa today with 2 transports and 3 other cans, headed for Pearl Harbor.

EWF: Dec 11/43

We arrived in Pearl Harbor today

EWF: Dec 13/43

They just announced we were going to Bremerton Washington. All of us are happy as h.

EWF: Dec 19/43

We arrived Bremerton this noon.

EWF: Dec 20/43

I start on leave today with 14 days. A miracle has happened.

[End of 1943 diary entries]

Notes and References

The Guadalcanal Campaign, begun in August 1942, finally concluded with the Japanese abandonment of the island in February 1943. It was one of the largest engagements of WW2 in the Pacific, and included massive ground, naval, and air battles; it marked a major strategic turning point in the US offensive against Japan.

In November 1943, Franklin D. Roosevelt, Winston Churchill, and Chiang Kai-shek met in Egypt to discuss how to defeat Japan. The result was a declaration "to restrain and punish the aggression of Japan", and to "procure the unconditional surrender of Japan".

Chapter 3: 1944

Timeline

1944

June

6	D-Day Invasion of Normandy
19	Major air battle in Marianas shoots down 220 Japanese aircraft
19-21	Battle of Philippine Sea

July

19	US Marines invade Guam

September

2	George H W Bush's Navy plane shot down

October

20	US troops land on Leyte
23-26	Naval Battle of Leyte Gulf
25	First major Kamikaze attacks
25	Destroyers *USS Hoel* (DD 533), *USS Johnston* (DD 557), and escort *USS Samuel B. Roberts* (DE 413) sunk during a raid against enemy battleships off the island of Samar. Only 86 of *Hoel's* complement survived while 253 officers and crew died with their ship.

Diary Entries and Ship Actions

EWF: Jan 1/44

I arrived in Seattle.

EWF: Jan 16/44

We left Bremerton and went to Seattle. Most of the boys think we will hit the east coast when we leave the States this time.

EWF: Jan 29/44

We finally left Seattle. Headed for San Pedro with the California and another can.

EWF: Feb 11/44

We finally left the States headed for Pearl Harbor.

EWF: Feb 16/44

Today we pulled into Pearl Harbor. Today the skipper got the "Legion of Merit" award for sinking the sub up off Kiska.

The President of the United States of America takes pleasure in presenting the Legion of Merit with Combat "V" to Lieutenant Commander Simon Everett Ramey (NSN: 0-78765), United States Navy, for exceptionally meritorious conduct in the performance of outstanding services to the Government of the United States as Commanding Officer of the Destroyer U.S.S. EDWARDS (DD-619) during a four-day running battle against enemy aircraft. Lieutenant Commander Ramey was constantly alert and by his efficient gunfire, shiphandling, radar warning and general assistance to the convoy, he contributed greatly to the protection of the convoy, to the destruction of thirty-seven enemy aircraft and to the damaging and driving off of many more. His meritorious actions throughout were in keeping with the highest traditions of the United States Naval Service. (Lieutenant Commander Ramey is authorized to wear the Combat "V".)

http://projects.militarytimes.com/citations-medals-awards/recipient.php?recipientid=56301

EWF: Mar 2/44

We left Pearl Harbor headed for the Marshall Islands

EWF: Mar 9/44

We pulled into Majuro in the Marshall Islands just 77 miles from a couple of jap air bases.

EWF: Mar 17/44

Got underway for Battleship and plane Bombardment of Mili Island. We have with us the New Jersey [1], Iowa, New

Lexington(?), and 7 other cans. We are to give the japs on Mili a good blasting.

EWF: Mar 18/44

The fireworks will start sometime this morning. The Battleships and 4 other cans left us in the night to bombard Mili. We will come up later with the carrier to bomb.

EWF: Mar 19/44

We pulled back into Majuro. The raid was successful. The japs fired back a little.

EWF: Mar 22/44

We got underway with a whole slue of ships this morning. We are to give the jap bases and units a lot of hell. We expect to be underway for 3 weeks. There is something big in the air. This is the biggest striking force of combatant ships any one nation has ever assembled.

EWF: Mar 25/44

We sure gave the pollywogs hell today.

EWF: Mar 29/44

Well this is it. We received this message from our task group commander. Our sea target is the jap fleet. Our land target is Palau Island just 500 miles east of the Philippines. We are in the heart of jap territory. The big day starts Thurs but we will gladly take them on any time.

EWF: Mar 29/44

This evening around 8:00 o'clock the japs attacked us. The battlewagon and A.A. cruiser in our force got one apiece. We fired at one but it was too dark to tell whether we got it or not. There were six groups of jap planes that came in on the Enterprise and her force. We could see a hellofa lot of firing but the planes never came within our reach.

NDWD: Mar 29/44

Repelled air attack, one plane shot down by USS Edwards (DD-619)

EWF: Mar 30/44

They started their raids on Palau Is. this morning. The planes reported 2 carriers, 1 cruiser, a couple of transports, some merchant ships, and a few other auxiliary ships sunk in the harbor. We still have a couple of days to go yet.

EWF: Mar 30/44

3:00 o'clock I'll make a correction to my last statement. We just received a message over the radio that <u>all</u> the shipping is burning, sinking or in a sinking condition. The airfields have been completely destroyed and the planes are preparing to bomb the hangars and another cruiser which is beached but still in good condition. There were cruisers cans transports carriers cargo ships and a lot of others which were all completely destroyed.

EWF: Mar 30/44

The japs attacked us again tonight. There were quite a few Bettys* that came in and all ships were firing.

* Twin-engine Japanese Mitsubishi G4M bombers

NDWD: Mar 30/44

Repelled enemy air attack, no planes downed, no damage.

EWF: Mar 31/44

The japs tried to get at us again this morning but our fighters met them out quite a ways and destroyed 9 of them. We got a report from the Mass. this noon that they seen the plane we fired at last night and they are sure we got it. Anyway we got credit for it. That makes (8) we have now.

EWF: Apr 1/44

We are going to give Woyla(?) a good blasting today. It is further north of Palau.

EWF: Apr 2/44

We start for the Barn(?)

EWF: Apr 3/44

We now have official credit for 2 more planes which brings to a grand total of 9 planes.

EWF: Apr 6/44

We arrive at last at Majuro.

EWF: Apr 12/44

We leave Majuro to give the japs another blasting.

EWF: Apr 22/44

We start this morning to give the jap airfields on New Guinea a work over. The place is called Hollandia.

EWF: Apr 22/44

This morning around 11:00 AM we picked up two men from a dive bomber. A pilot and the radioman. Both were hurt pretty bad. The pilot was given one chance out of a hundred to pull through. In other words he was about 95% gone. We got a surgeon from the Hornet to operate.

56

EWF: Apr 22/44

The pilot died in the night. We buried him at sea around 10:30.

EWF: Apr 23,24,25/44

For the last 3 days the japs have been sending out snoopers to get our position. Every day the fighters would shoot them down.

EWF: Apr 26/44

The carriers are going in to some port in the Admiralty group to get more planes.

EWF: Apr 29/44

Tomorrow morning we make an attack on Truk.

EWF: May 7/44

We pull in to Kwajalein in the Marshalls group.

EWF: May 9/44

We left Kwajalein and went to Majuro.

EWF: May 11/44

We left Majuro to patrol around Juliet

EWF: May 13/44

Tonight B-24s are bombing Juliet

EWF: May 15/44

We got a report today that there was a sub beached on one of the islands. We went in to investigate but we seen nothing. We did notice a pier with some barges tied up to it. We also saw some radio antenna.

EWF: May 23/44

We, the Edwards and Bancroft commence bombarding Wotje Island. While the Bancroft was firing we saw the japs open up with their shore batteries. We opened up on them and eliminated the gun position with our fourth salvo. I could hear those shells whistling just above the Directors. If we hadn't been zigzagging we probably would have been hit. They were falling all around us. 2:15 We are through bombarding and we go to patrol around another jap base until the 29th.

EWF: May 29/44

We pull into Majuro

EWF: May 31/44

We go out for patrol and gunnery exercises.

EWF: Jun 7/44

We pulled back into Majuro

EWF: Jun 9/44

We pulled out for patrol around Moelealap(?). We got word that there were 2 planes shot down over the lagoon and we were to go in and pick them up. The Frazier instead sent her motor whale boat in. They picked up the men while we covered them.

EWF: Jun 18/44

We returned to Majuro

EWF: Jun 20/44

We pulled out for patrol around Wotje

EWF: Jun 27/44

As we were patrolling our area some Corsairs came flying low over us. We saw him motion to us to to follow him. We got the word from a Catalina flying boat that a Corsair had been shot down about 4000 yd from the beach. While the Catalina was flying low over the water, dipping to show our whale boat where the plane was, the Catalina itself went into the drink. We got 7 men in all. The pilot of the Corsair was none other than George Frank, the All American football star [**].

NDWD: Jun 27/44

   While patrolling off Wotje a Marine Corsair crashed into the water off the island. The USS Edwards (DD-619) proceeded to area to effect rescue. A PBY "dumbo" attempting rescue crashed and sank. The ship's boat was launched, and in the face of shore fire all aviators were rescued without casualty. For this action the following men were awarded the Navy and Marine Corps Medal for heroism: Lieutenant (jg) Franklin Harold MANN, USNR (187641); Emery PENSAK, 328-84-47, CPhM(AA), USN; Frank Andrew Stein ELLIOTT, 642-03-71, MoMMlc, USNR; John Joseph CRANE, 207-39-68, Cox, USN; and Richard STANLEY, 852-25-33, Slc, USNR.

EWF: Jun 28/44

   We pulled into Majuro and put the pilots.

EWF: Jun 30/44

   We pulled out for patrol around Juliet

EWF: Jul 5/44

   We pulled in to Majuro

EWF: Jul 7/44

   We pulled out for patrol around Wotje. Boy the patrol duty is getting damned monotonous.

EWF: Jul 8/44

We left patrol around Wotje and started for Eniwetok. Maybe we're with patrol for a while.

EWF: Jul 9/44

We pulled in to Eniwetok.

EWF: Jul 10/44

We pulled out this morning to escort the Enterprise to the 170th Meridian. The Enterprise got a fish in her around Saipan.

EWF: Jul 11/44

We pulled back into Eniwetok

EWF: Jul 17/44

We pull out today escorting a floating dry dock and several tugs deep into enemy territory. Which means we're going to Saipan.

EWF: Jul 24/44

We pulled in to Saipan. We sat in the harbor and watched them load and bombard the beach at Tinian. They are still fighting to beat h.

EWF: Jul 25/44

We will return to Eniwetok at 10:00 today. (The remainder of this diary is in another book) [2]

EWF: Aug 2/44

We pulled out with a transport. We will escort it for (2) days and pull into Majuro

EWF: Aug 5/44

We pull in to Majuro

EWF: Aug 6/44

We pull out for some infernal patrol.

EWF: Aug 7/44

We get word that the Caldwell had a sub contact around Mili. We leave patrol around Juliet for hunter killer patrol for 24 hrs.

EWF: Aug 11/44

We returned to Majuro

EWF: Aug 14/44

We pull out for our last patrol around Wotje. When we're through with this patrol we will head for Pearl Harbor.

EWF: Aug 18/44

We pull into Majuro

EWF: Aug 19/44

About 5:30 PM we pull out for P.H.T.H.*

* Pearl Harbor, Territory of Hawaii

EWF: Aug 24/44

We arrive in Pearl Harbor

EWF: Sep 15/44

We pull out for trial runs.

EWF: Sep 16/44

We pull back in to P.H.

EWF: Sep 17/44

We pull out with the West Virginia and Hancock headed for the Admiralty Islands.

EWF: Sep 24/44

We pull into Manos Island in the Admiralties

EWF: Oct 9/44

We pull out alone headed for Hollandia in New Guinea.

EWF: Oct 10/44

We arrive in Hollandia

20 OCT: US troops land in Philippines

EWF: Oct 26/44

We pull out of Hollandia headed for Leyte in the Philippines. There are with us two hospital transports and two D.E.'s *

* Destroyer Escorts

The Kamikazes

The Battle of Leyte Gulf in the Philippine Islands, from October 23 through 26, was one of the largest naval battles in history. It unfolded during General Douglas MacArthur's invasion of Leyte Island, and involved most of the remaining capital ships of the Japanese Imperial Navy against the US Navy, as well as hundreds of smaller ships and thousands of aircraft. As the Japanese began losing the battle, having lost several aircraft carriers and battleships, they turned to an unexpected and horrific tactic that at first surprised and terrified US sailors -- the Kamikaze suicide attacks. Japanese planes of all types were filled with explosives and their pilots attempted to crash them into the American ships. Although many of the attackers were shot down or missed their targets completely, a large number were successful, severely damaging and often sinking them. At the Leyte Gulf battle, Kamikaze attacks crippled or sank dozens of Navy ships, including the carrier USS St Lo, the first major US vessel to fall prey to the suicide tactics.

Foreground: A late model Ohka 22 (1945) "Flying Bomb" designed for Kamikaze attacks; earlier models were dropped from Japanese Navy bombers and aimed at Allied warships. Background: Nakajima J1N1 twin-engine fighter, also used in Kamikaze attacks.
Author's photo of planes on display at the Smithsonian's Udvar-Hazy National Air and Space Museum in Chantilly, Virginia.

Japan, desperate to protect its homeland and to inflict as much damage to the Americans as possible, continued with the Kamikaze attacks for the remainder of the war; nearly 4000 such attacks were attempted, with nearly 20% hitting their targets. And although many such attacks were unsuccessful, their psychological effect was formidable; US sailors were astonished that so many Japanese were willing to die in that manner. As these attacks were underway, they were often characterized as an epic, mortal struggle "between those determined to live and those determined to die".

The first targets of the suicide attacks were often the destroyers on "radar picket duty" (early warning) surrounding and protecting the larger carriers, battleships, and heavy cruisers. These destroyers, which included the **USS Edwards**, along with heavy fighter aircraft support, frequently saw the heaviest Kamikaze attacks and casualties. In the naval battle at Okinawa in the Spring of 1945, for example, *ten* US destroyers were sunk and more than 30 damaged.

EWF: Oct 29/44

We pull into Leyte at 6:47. About 9:00 o'clock we go to GQ. The japs pulled a suicide attack but P38s took care of them before they got over the harbor. At 5:30 and 10:00 (p.m.) the japs came back again.

EWF: Oct 30/44

We had another air raid this morning this noon and again tonight.

EWF: Oct 31/44 & Nov 1/44

The japs came in again about 4 different times. This time they must have hit an oil dump on the beach because there was a heck of a big fire. In all 4 raids the P38s shot down 4 planes (2

in one attack) over the harbor. As a total they shot down from 30 to 35.

EWF: Nov 1/44

At about 3:00 P.M. today we received word that there was a jap task force consisting of 2 BBs, 4 to 6 CLs, and 8 or 10 DDs. They were reported 500 or 600 miles south west of us. They were no doubt headed our way to try and get into Leyte Harbor. We took the place of another can in Task Force 71 who was badly damaged. We received word that the japs has pulled and air raid on another force. They sunk the Abner Reed and badly damaged 5 or 6 more cans (Tiller, Ammon, Anderson). The force we are with now consists of 3 BB, 4 cruisers, and from 10 to 12 cans.

EWF: Nov 2/44

We received word that the japs had a couple of CLs, 7 or 8 cans and about 4 transports. They were bringing in reinforcements to the western side of Leyte.

EWF: Nov 6/44

The jap task force that was south of us has been lost. We don't know what they are up to yet.

EWF: Nov 12/44

The japs attacked again. They set two Liberty ships afire. 7 or 9 of the planes were shot down. I seen one as a P38 started pouring slugs into it. Boy what a lovely flame it made.

EWF: Nov 27/44

Again the task group was attacked by suicide bombers. One crashed into the St. Louis (CC) and the Colorado (BB). Minor damage as a result.

EWF: Nov 28/44

A lone jap plane tried a suicide dive on the Portland (CL) but was shot down.

EWF: Nov 29/44

The japs sent another suicide force over. One of them crashed on the Maryland but no damage was caused. Two can on (B.C.) patrol got damaged a little. One took a plane with bombs intact. She also lost her radar. The other one got hit by a suicide dive bomber. The Ross, which was already damaged, was in a floating dry dock. A plane strafed it and then dove into it. Several were injured.

EWF: Dec 3/44

I just got word that another can, the Cooper was sunk over in Ormoc Bay last night and two other cans were damaged.

The Army was suppose to give them air coverage while they were looking for ships but they didn't get it.

EWF: Dec 6/44

About 5:00 we pull out and head down (?) Strait. There was a force of landing crafts and about 11 cans. We are supposed to join them and then head for Ormoc Bay where we will land troops on the west side of Leyte. At about 6:00 as we were going to join up with the force there were at least 40 Sallys (jap bombers) headed up the strait. We opened fire on them and got one and maybe damaged two. We later got the word that their mission was to land parachute troops and also bomb our airfields. Practically all were shot down but they succeeded in landing about 200 which were all killed.

NDWD: Dec 6/44

...At 1811 in the vicinity of Amagusan Point took under fire very large group of enemy planes. Shot down one SALLY. Planes later identified as those carrying Japanese Paratroops...

EWF: Dec 7/44 [3]

Thursday will be a day I'll never forget. Things have happened so fast that I won't attempt to put down any time. The japs were coming in on us all day long. We succeeded in landing our troops with hardly any casualties. The japs came at us while our second wave was going in. They suicide dived two of our ships one on (a p.d) the Ward(?) and a can the Mahan. An LCI was bombed and we went along side to take off the casualties. While we were along side the japs attacked us again.

(Dinah) jap twin engine bombers and (Vals) (jap) came in again. This time one suicide plane hit an (LST) and (2) planes crashed into a can the Lamson. We came 2 damn close to being crash dived. I don't even like to think about it. We received credit for 5 of those that came in.

We were all through and starting back when our can was attacked by a (Judy). We and the Smith fired on it. The P38s were also on his tail. He finally came down. All together we have official count for 14 (fourteen) planes.

NDWD: Dec 7/44

...1441 Took under fire five HAPS or ZEKES. Three planes shot down by USS Edwards (DD-619). One plane attempted suicide dive on ship, and clipped off stern light before crashing into sea. 1545 JUDY sighted diving on ship and was shot down. 1615 Took under fire two JUDYS one shot down by USS Edwards (DD-619), later, shot at unidentified planes closing from the stern and drove them off. THE END OF A HECTIC DAY.

EWF: Dec 11/44

We pull out again headed for Ormoc Bay with (LCIs) and (LSTs) to carry troops and supplies to the Army on the west side of Leyte. At about 5:45 or 6:00 o'clock the japs came in on us. A suicide plane and a bomb sank one of our cans the Reid. They also strafed us.

NDWD: Dec 11/44

...1700 sighted 10 single engine planes dead ahead. Planes sank USS REID (DD-369).

EWF: Dec 12/44

On our way back the japs attacked us again in the afternoon. We got about 4 or five misses with bombs. The Caldwell was bombed and also took a suicide plane.

NDWD: Dec 12/44

0005 Snoopers in vicinity. 0405 convoy commenced retirement. 0623 attacked by three enemy planes, no hits. 0756 sighted 22 enemy planes approaching planes attacked. 0810 USS CALDWELL (DD-605) hit by suicider. 0830 attack subsided. 0925 took aboard some USS CALDWELL (DD-605) casualties...For the action on 11-12 Dec. the Commanding Officer, Lieut. S.E. RAMEY, USN received the Silver Star Medal.

EWF: Dec 14/44

The cruiser Nashville came in today. She had been bombed and crash dived buy the japs while with a convoy that was headed for Mindoro.

EWF: Dec 15/44

Up to date the japs have really been raising hell with us. They have either damaged or sunk a great toll of our cans. And every time we go out I have a feeling that they might get us next. I pray to God that they don't.

EWF: Dec 24/44

Our Xmas Eve over, the japs won't leave us alone. They have been almost every night up to date.

EWF: Dec 25/44

Well, even if I didn't have any this day [4] I at least had a damn swell dinner, considering.

EWF: Dec 26/44

I heard that two cans got it last night and also a minesweeper they were escorting. The minesweeper was and almost all hands were killed. One of the cans were fished and the other was crashed by a suicide plane. Us and about 7 other cans are going to leave soon for Mindoro with a convoy of over a (100) hundred ships. We are promised air coverage.

EWF: Dec 28/44

We pull out with a very large convoy to resupply Mindoro.

EWF: Dec 28/44

Around 10:00 o'clock we were attacked by jap dive bombers. An LST, an LCI, and an ammunition ship were sunk. The ammunition ship went sky high and it no doubt took a couple of small craft with it. One merchant ship was crash dived. They came at us again around 11:30 and another wave at twilight.

NDWD: Dec 28/44

1011 Sighted six enemy planes approaching for attack. 1017 open fire on diving plane. 1839 sighted four enemy planes closing. 1842 commenced firing, 1855 shot one plane down in flames. 1915 shot down two engined plane close aboard to stbd. 1930 ordered to assist the damaged LST 750.

After clearing the ship of wounded, and seeing that salvage was impossible, sank the LST by gunfire at 2329.

EWF: Dec 29/44

They made another stab at us today but no damage was done. We shot down two planes on this night. We also were ordered to go back and sink one of our LSTs that had been fished but didn't sink.

NDWD: Dec 29/44

Rejoined group after sinking LST. 0726 fired on four planes over formation, no hits. 0814 opened fire on attacking planes.

74

Straddled by bombs, but no hits, 1702 four to six planes dropped bombs at ships without any hits. 1703 fired at attacking planes. 1910 main attack over, harassing attacks continued throughout the night.

EWF: Dec 30/44

We arrived at Mindoro around 7:30. The japs came at us again. One of those yellow rats came so damn close to sinking us that I had almost told myself we were goners. He came diving straight at us and we poured everything we had at him but didn't stop him. He let his bomb go when he was about 50 feet from the ship. It landed almost flat and skipped just over amidships. That was the closest call we've ever had. [5]

NDWD: Dec 30/44

0652 Single plane attacks commenced. 1543 opened fire on VAL attacking ship. This plane dropped his bomb which landed short of the ship SKIPPED OVER IT, and fell on the other side of the ship in the water almost knocking down the VAL.

AR: 30 DEC 44

Opened fire on a VAL making an attack on this ship from the east. This plane approached on a 20 degree power glide using sidewise jinking maneuvers and porpoising to avoid gunfire. His bomb, release early, landed about 25 yards to starboard, ricocheted, and tumbled over the the ship at masthead height. The plane barely cleared his own bomb as he zoomed over, still in his glide. After pulling out this plane circled back, obviously for a crash attempt, but was successfully driven off, disappearing to westward. During this attack the USS GANSEVOORT (DD608) and two other ships were hit by suicide planes.

EWF: Dec 31/44

We at least had some peace all day today. And the night was the same.

[End of 1944 diary entries]

Notes and References

[1] "USS *New Jersey* was the only WW2 battleship recalled to duty during the Vietnam War. She recommissioned in April 1968 and arrived off Southeast Asia in September. From then until April 1969, she conducted frequent bombardments along the South Vietnamese coast." http://www.history.navy.mil/our-collections/photography/us-navy-ships/battleships/new-jersey-bb-62.html

Author's note: During my tour in Vietnam with the Army's *First Infantry Division*, my unit on occasion called in artillery fire from the New Jersey's big 16-inch guns.

[2] Author's note: This second diary book was less well preserved and more difficult to transcribe. Some of the pencil text was very faint and had to be illuminated with UV light to render it readable.

[3] On the top of page 67 in the diary is written "Dates to remember. Louise – Sept 16". This is the date of Louise Bodner's birthday, whom Earl married after the war. This entry was probably not written on Dec 7/44 but added at a later date.

[4] Author's note: I assume he meant "no attackers".

[5] Family lore / Author's note: I don't recall my father talking much about his wartime experiences, but he did occasionally refer to this one incident.

[**] George Franck: http://www.sports-reference.com/cfb/players/george-franck-1.html, and http://goldenrankings.com/nflchampionshipgame1946.html

Chapter 4: 1945

Timeline

1945

January
9	American troops land on Luzon, Philippines

February
3	US attacks Manila
19	US Marines attack Iwo Jima

March
9-10	US B-29s firebomb Tokyo, estimated 100,000 deaths
18	First Oka Kamikaze attacks

April
1	Allies invade Okinawa
6	*USS Bush* (DD 529), *USS Colhoun* (DD 801) and other vessels sunk after Japanese kamikazes attacked them off the coast of Okinawa. Both the *Bush* and *Colhoun* shot down several Japanese planes during the attack.
7	Japanese battleship Yamato sunk
12	President FDR dies, Harry Truman becomes President
16	USS Pringle (DD 477) sunk and USS Laffey (DD 724) was heavily damaged by six aircraft and four bombs during a kamikaze attack off of Okinawa. Laffey had all of her gun turrets destroyed and lost 103 men during the attack.
30	Hitler commits suicide

May
3	USS Little (DD 803), USS Luce (DD 522) and the USS Morrison (DD 560) sank after a kamikaze attack of 124 planes off of Okinawa.
7	Germany surrenders
8	Victory in Europe Day
11	USS carrier Bunker Hill hit and disabled by 2 Kamikazes, 400 men lost

July
16	First atomic bomb test ("Trinity")
30	USS Indianapolis sunk [1]

August
6	Atomic bombing of Hiroshima (78,000 killed)
9	Atomic bombing of Nagasaki (24,000 killed)
15	Emperor Hirohito announces Japan surrender

September
2	Formal surrender of Japan aboard USS Missouri in Tokyo Bay; VJ Day (Victory over Japan)

October
27	US Navy Day Celebration, NYC

Diary Entries and Ship Actions

EWF: Jan 1/45

We had a little fireworks this morning. A snooper came prowling around the convoy. He must have spotted the fighters because he let his bombs go quite a ways from the formation and crossed over just about the middle of us. The fighters shot him down.

EWF: Jan 4/45

We pull out for the invasion of Luzon. We have with us (4) cruisers and 8 cans. Behind us is the invasion force. "D" day is the ninth. Note: We now have a grand total of 17 planes. During the Mindoro operation the Gansevoort and about 3 merchant ships were hit, also an LST. A force that was a good ways ahead of us was attacked by torpedo planes. A carrier(?) was damaged and had to be sunk.

AR: 5 JAN 45

Proceeded through Mindanao Sea without incident until 1435 when unidentified planes were reported. 1514 After air alert had ended, torpedo wake sighted approaching formation from the north. Two minutes later TAYLOR sighted a periscope. TAYLOR and NICHOLAS designated to destroy submarine. 1527 TAYLOR rammed partially surfaced midget submarine and followed with full depth charge pattern, submarine probably destroyed.

EWF: Jan 7/45

A Dinah flew over us this morning and dropped a bomb but it was a good ways away from any of the ships. Another came around about 9:30 and was shot down by the fighters.

EWF: Jan 8/45

The japs came at us this morning, there were quite a few shot down by our fighters. They came at us again tonight, about 4 Vals and 3 or 4 Judies. A carrier was damaged, a transport got a near miss by a plane. We also got a near miss, no damage.

EWF: Jan 9/45

Today is "D" day. At about 7:25 McArthur gave the word to start loading the barges. And about 9:45 the troops started hitting the beach. The japs came at us this morning. they crashed the Columbia with one plane. They also came at us this evening. The Miss and Australia was crash dived. That makes about 5 that the Australia has had. The New Mexico also caught five planes. But hardly any damage was caused to either ship. They came at us again tonight with planes and PT boats. They sunk an LCI and badly damaged a transport and can.

EWF: Jan 10/45

They came at us 3 or 4 times today. Tonight a dive bomber crashed a transport. And during this morning the transports over (?) to Blue beach were reporting japs in the water with high explosives tied to them or either with hand grenades trying to damage or sink our ships. They killed (9) that tried that.

EWF: Jan 11/45

They came at us again tonight and damaged our APD(?)

EWF: Jan 12/45

They came at us again once or twice today. We sure got a near miss and we thought for a moment that we had some holes in our side but no damage was done.

EWF: Jan 13/45

We pull out tonight with the Boise and Chaglon(?). We join up with a carrier and cruiser force. We are to supply air coverage around Luzon until their airfields pretty well advanced.

EWF: Jan 21/45

We pull into Mindoro to take on ammo and fuel. Our next operation is the 30th Jan. We are going to land troops on Northern Luzon. But we aren't in on it. This can has been through more attacks than any other can in the Philippines. And we have also been out here in this area longer than any others.

EWF: Jan 22/45

We leave Mindoro and join a convoy headed for Luzon.

EWF: Jan 27/45

We pull into Lingayen with the resupply force.

EWF: Jan 28/45

We, the Chaglon(?), and a few other cans start back to Leyte with a 12 knot convoy.

EWF: Jan 31/45

We pull in to Tacloban for the night.

AR: 31 JAN 45

Although the officers and crew of this ship have been in continuous contact with the enemy since 29 October 1944 without opportunity for physical or mental relaxation, they continued to perform their duties in a calm, courageous and efficient manner which is in keeping with the highest traditions of US Naval Service.

EWF: Feb 1/45

We pull into Leyte, we expect to be here til the 5th.

EWF: Feb 8/45

We pull out with a convoy headed for Luzon.

EWF: Feb 13/45

>We pull into Lingayen Gulf in Luzon.

EWF: Feb 13/45

>We haven't had an alert for quit some time now. Everything must be pretty well under control.

EWF: Feb 14/45

>We are assigned to the harbor patrol unit. We may be called on at any time to go out on sub patrol or investigate targets or fire a few star shells over jap held positions.

EWF: Mar 26/45

>At last we have received our mail that we have been waiting well over two months for.

EWF: Apr 5/45

>We leave Lingayen and head for Subic Bay.

EWF: Apr 6/45

>We arrive at Subic Bay.

EWF: Apr 19/45

>5:30 am We leave Subic with the Blue Ridge and head for Manila.

EWF: Apr 19/45

1:00 pm We arrive at Manila and anchor in the Bay.

EWF: Apr 22/45

We leave Manila with the Blue Ridge and late in the afternoon pull into Subic Bay.

EWF: Apr 24/45

18:00 We pull out of Subic and head for Mindoro.

EWF: Apr 25/45

07:30 We pull into Mindoro. We will pull out again at noon with 3 other cans and 30 or 40 LSIs for resupplying troops on Mindanao.

EWF: Apr 29/45

We arrive at Mindanao. We anchor in Bay at Parang.

EWF: Apr 30/45

We pull out to take supplies and fresh troops to a point 20 miles south of Davao.

EWF: May 2/45

We reach our destination. The LCIs commence unloading and we start back to Parang.

EWF: May 3/45

    3:45 We arrive at Parang.

EWF: May 5/45

    About 4:15 We pull out with supplies and troops for Davao.

EWF: May 6/45

    We arrive at Davao with our convoy. We were told to look over a point a little East of Davao. There was supposed to have been a midget sub base there but we could locate nothing.

EWF: May 6/45

    Will pull out of Davao. Tonight we leave the convoy with a tug and head for Tarakan right next to Borneo.

EWF: May 11/45

    We pull into Tarakan

EWF: May 12/45

    We are suppose to lend fire support to the Dutch and Aussies tonight.

EWF: May 13/45

    We expended (500) rounds at jap positions just a little East of Tarakan.

EWF: May 13/45

We pull out with a convoy of LSTs, headed for Morotai

EWF: May 16/45

We arrive at Morotai

EWF: Jun 4/45

About 11:30 o'clock we pull out for an invasion, somewhere around Borneo [sic]. We have a hell of a big force. We're supposed to invade at Brunei Bay on the West coast of Borneo.

EWF: Jun 10/45

We start through the channel into Brunei Bay. At about 3:45 or 4:00 we are inside Brunei Bay. We wait around until 9:15 to start landing troops. At about 6:30 – 7:00 there was one lone plane that dropped his bomb near a transport but no damage was done. Except for that one plane everything has been nice and quiet all morning and things going along just as planned.

EWF: Jun 12/45

They just released news that all the troops got ashore after a heavy bombardment and met no opposition. The japs had taken to the hills.

EWF: Jun 12/45

We pull out about 12:00 with a div. of minesweepers. We are supposed to join up with two more cans and more minesweepers.

EWF: Jun 14/45

We joined up with the other cans and minesweepers late last night. This morning we start to sweep the area assigned to us. The minesweepers are raising a hell of a lot of mines and we are supposed to give them support fire when they get in close to the beach. We destroyed two (2) jap (AA) positions on the beach. We start back at 8:00.

EWF: Jun 15/45

We arrive at Brunei Bay around 7:30. We will patrol the rest of the day and go in tomorrow and become(SOPA)*

* Senior Officer Present Afloat

EWF: Jun 16/45

We go in today and take on Captain Husson(?) and his staff. We will be senior ship around here until July 11.

EWF: Jul 11/45

We pull out with one LST headed for Subic Bay.

EWF: Jul 15/45

We pull into Subic Bay. We will conduct shore bombardment from now until the 18th.

EWF: Jul 28/45

We leave Subic and proceed to Manila so the crew could get liberty.

EWF: Jul 32/45

We leave Manila and proceed to Subic and await further orders.

EWF: Jul 32/45

We pull into Subic late at noon.

EWF: Aug 12/45

We leave Subic bay and arrive at Manila around noon. We are here for escort duty.

EWF: Aug 14/45

We get underway at 9:00 this morning. We are to take a communications ship to Iwo Jima. If the war is over before we get to Iwo, then we will proceed further into Japan. If not then we will await further orders at Iwo.

EWF: Aug 15, 1945

At 8:07 this morning we received word that Truman had announced the war was over, Japan had accepted the counter(?) surrender terms. As soon as we hit port we are going to break out the beer and raise hell. So ends the war.

EWF: Aug 18/45

We pull into Iwo Jima. This afternoon we will celebrate V-J day. We will have all the chow and ice cream we can eat and entertainment on the forecastle.

EWF: Aug 24/45

We leave Iwo Jima and start back for Subic.

EWF: Aug 25/45

We arrive at Subic.

[Last daily entry of Earl's diary]

Notes and References

World War II was the bloodiest war in human history, with more than 40 million deaths: http://www.britannica.com/event/World-War-II. More than 100,000 US servicemen died in the Pacific phase of the war, and more than 2 million Japanese servicemen.

To date, the only use of atomic weapons in warfare was the bombings of Hiroshima and Nagasaki in August 1945: https://en.wikipedia.org/wiki/Atomic_bombings_of_Hiroshima_and_Nagasaki

Epilog

The final page of Earl's diary lists six song titles:

- I'll Get By
- I'll Be Seeing You
- Long Ago and Far Away
- Amor
- Time Waits for No One
- Good Night Wherever You Are

Why he chose these song titles to record is unclear; all of them were popular during the early 1940's, many of them favorites of soldiers and sailors far from home at the time.

After the war Earl returned to civilian life, and married Louise Bodner. He worked at various companies as a machinist. His children included Amy Louise Foxwell, Jean Paul Foxwell, and Harry Joseph Foxwell.

Fate of the USS Edwards DD-619:

7 Jan 1946: USS Edwards arrives at Charleston, SC

11 Apr 1946: USS Edwards placed out of commission in reserve

1 Jul 1971: USS Edwards stricken from the Navy

25 May 1973: USS Edwards sold and broken up for scrap.

Appendix

EWF & DD-619 Itinerary from undated diary insert

Place names' spellings have been corrected if known.

(?) indicates illegible or unknown reference.

1. New York
2. Portland, Me
3. New York
4. Norfolk
5. St. Thomas, V.I.
6. San Juan, Porto Rico
7. Trinidad
8. Bermuda
9. New York
10. Norfolk
11. Colon, Panama
12. Balboa
13. New Caledonia, Noumea
14. New Hebrides
15. Guadalcanal
16. Pearl Harbor
17. Adak, Alaska
18. Attu
19. Cold Bay, Alaska
20. Inv. (Invasion) of Attu
21. Kiska
22. Amchitka
23. Adak
24. Kiska
25. San Francisco
26. Brimston (?), WA

27. Pearl Harbor

28. Espiritu Santo

29. Bougainville

30. Rabaul

31. Rabaul "(Nov.11th)"

32. (?) Is.

33. Gilberts

34. Tarawa

35. Pearl Harbor

36. Bremerton, Wash

37. San Pedro

38. Pearl Harbor

39. Majuro

40. R(?)

41. W(?)

42. Majuro

43. Hollandia

44. Truk

45. Ponape

46. K(?)

47. Jaluit

48. (?)

49. Eniwetok

50. Saipan

51. Tinian

52. Majuro

53. Jaluit

54. W(?)

55. Pearl Harbor

56. Manus Is.

57. Hollandia

58. Leyte, P.I.

59. Ormoc Bay

60. Mindanao

61. Lingayen Gulf

62. Leyte

63. Lingayen

64. Subic Bay

65. Parang

66. Morotai

67. Ta(?)

68. Morotai

69. Borneo

70. Subic Bay

71. Manila

72. Subic Bay

73. Iwo Jima ("End of War, Aug 14, 1945")

74. Subic Bay

75. Eniwetok

76. Pearl Harbor

77. San Pedro

78. Colon

79. Balboa

80. Brooklyn Navy Yard

81. Newark

82. Brooklyn Navy Yard

"Transferred Dec 10, 1945"

About the Author

Harry J. Foxwell is a computer systems engineer for the Oracle Corporation in Reston, Virginia, and an Adjunct Professor of Computer Science for George Mason University in Fairfax, Virginia. He is also a combat veteran, having served in Viet Nam in the US Army's First Infantry Division in 1968-1969. His wartime experience is included in Peter Goldman's book, *Charlie Company: What Vietnam Did to Us*, http://www.petergoldman.com/charlie_company_what_vietnam_d id_to_us_114410.htm.

He is the coauthor of three books on computer operating systems, and the author/coauthor of numerous technical papers.

He lives with his wife, Eileen, in Fairfax, Virginia.